....

A GIFT TO

....

FROM

....

ON THIS DATE

KEEPING GOD IN THE SMALL STUFF

25 DEVOTIONS *for* EVERYDAY

bruce & stan

A DayMaker Greeting Book

LITTLE IS MUCH IF GOD IS IN IT

Do not despise these small beginnings,

for the LORD rejoices to see the work begin.

ZECHARIAH 4:10 NLT

A national best-selling book suggests that you shouldn't sweat the small stuff. Many people treat the small stuff in life as if no one—not even God—has any control over what happens. They call it "fate" or talk about how they are "lucky" or "fortunate" when certain things happen or don't happen.

We're not suggesting that you should involve God in every decision you make no matter how small (for example, you don't have to ask God what you should wear in the morning). But if you're like most people, you tend to ask for God's involvement only in times of major need or crisis, and consequently you miss out on the joy and wonder of watching God work in the small stuff of your life. There's no question God is in the big events, but He delights in working in the details.

KEEP THE TRUTH TOGETHER

People with integrity have firm footing,

but those who follow crooked paths will slip and fall.

PROVERBS 10:9 NLT

Telling the truth has become a lost art. It's not that we're out there telling lies (although there is plenty of that going on). We're just not telling "the truth, the whole truth, and nothing but the truth." We sort of sneak up on the truth, circle the truth, tell part of the truth, but don't come right out and tell the whole truth. We give out just enough information to keep us out of trouble, but not enough to honor God.

When God asks us to be truthful, He isn't suggesting that we pick out the parts that make us look good. He wants us to deal in whole truth. That's what it means to have integrity: to be "whole." If you want to be a person of integrity, don't break the truth into pieces. Keep it together, even if it invites criticism.

Do What Is Good

Motivation can fade.

Habits prevail.

Every now and then, we need to hear a great motivational sermon. It can really recharge our spiritual batteries. But you must avoid becoming a motivational junkie—the kind of person who has to be hyped up emotionally before you can get going. If you become dependent on motivational sermons, you'll fail miserably in your spiritual life. (You'll get weary of the emotional roller coaster. And after a while, all of the sermons will sound the same.)

Instead of depending on someone else to fire you up, get busy helping others. Do it regularly. Make it a part of your life. When "doing good" for others is a habit in your life, then you'll find that it happens regardless of your emotions. You'll find that you're doing these things because they are rewarding (not just because some eloquent speaker psyched you into it).

GRAB THE TOWEL

Be more concerned about the task to

be performed by you than the title to

be conferred upon you.

Remember the story of Jesus washing the feet of the disciples? (See John 13:1–11.) It was the custom to wash the feet of guests who had been traveling on the dusty roads. The disciples weren't doing the job, so Jesus got busy and did the task Himself. What makes this incident so ironic is that the disciples had been arguing earlier about which of them was going to be "greatest" in God's Kingdom. While they were worried about a title, Jesus grabbed the towel.

We can't be too critical of the disciples, because we make the same mistake. We're so anxious to be important, to be noticed, and to have prestige. We're thinking so much about our own image that we overlook the needs of others.

Let Jesus be your example. Forget about your own self-importance and focus on the needs of others. Be looking for ways that you can be helpful.

YOUR FAMILY

Love one another.

1 JOHN 4:7 NLT

Hospitality is often defined as the display of thoughtfulness to strangers and guests. But having guests over for dinner is only part of hospitality—the easy part. The more challenging aspect of hospitality happens after the door shuts when the visitors leave: Can your family treat each other with the same attention and respect that is reserved for special visitors?

We are often more kind to strangers and friends than we are to the members of our family. The "outsiders" get the best part of us, while the people in our own household get the worst part of us. There's an old saying that goes, "Familiarity breeds contempt," but it doesn't have to be true just because it is old.

Here's another old saying: "I command you to love each other" (John 15:17). When Jesus said these words, He didn't exclude those with whom you share a bathroom and refrigerator.

GOD'S WHISPER

If you aren't hearing the voice of God,

your life may be too noisy.

People often wonder if God ever speaks in a voice we can hear. Absolutely. There are times when God speaks through other people in order to tell us something. And sometimes God will speak directly to us. So how do we listen to the voice of God?

If we want to hear God's voice, the first thing we need to be is quiet. God won't shout above the cacophony of our lives. As the prophet Elijah discovered, God comes quietly when we least expect Him. God told Elijah to meet Him "on the mountain" (1 Kings 19:11). As Elijah waited, there was a mighty windstorm, an earthquake, and a fire, but the Lord wasn't in any of those. He came to Elijah in "a gentle whisper."

God will come to you in a gentle whisper, too—in your thoughts and in your heart. But you'll never hear God's voice unless you turn off the noise.

LOVE BEFORE FIRST SIGHT

God loved you long before
you loved Him.

Hollywood movie producers know that the romantic notion of "love at first sight" makes for a good love story. In real life, however, it is nothing more than "attraction at first sight." Real love requires knowing a person.

God didn't love you at first sight, because He actually loved you long before you were born. In fact, He loved you before He created the world. Since before the beginning of time, God knew all about you. He has known all along the kind of person you would be. Even though He has known forever all of your weaknesses, He has loved from then until now.

Don't ever think that God loves you because you have decided to love Him. Your love definitely pleases Him, but He is not reciprocating your affection. God has been loving you and awaiting your affection throughout history. Now that's a love story.

SORROW

When God gives us forgiveness,

Satan gives us guilt.

There is a fine line between sorrow and guilt. Both emotions can spring from doing something wrong. But the consequences of these two emotions can be drastically different.

God wants you to be sorry when you have done something wrong. Sincere sorrow is part of the process of repentance. It means you regret what you have done and don't want to do it again. With this type of attitude, God can turn your life around and get you back on the right track.

Satan, on the other hand, wants you to go far beyond sorrow. He wants you to feel guilty, and he uses guilt as an oppressive emotion. It will make your conscience heavy and your focus introspective. Guilt ignores the very reason why Jesus died for you: forgiveness.

The next time you regret your actions, thank God. Your sorrow is a sign that Jesus is alive and active in your life.

INTEGRITY

If you expand the truth,

your credibility contracts.

You know you shouldn't lie, but there are circumstances in life when the truth may seem irrelevant. Is absolute honesty required at all times? Are you obligated to limit your promises to the ones you actually intend to keep? Must you restrict your comments to those that are entirely truthful?

The culture in Jesus' time was so accustomed to making false statements that people would often "swear" to be telling the truth. They assumed that taking an oath of honesty would give greater credibility to their statements. Jesus. . .taught that integrity and truth have only one level (Matthew 5:33–37).

Your word should be enough. Jesus wants your words to be truthful in every conversation. Honesty, integrity, and truthfulness should be more than mere concepts for you. God wants you to put them into practice, and He wants them to be defining characteristics of your life.

GET ON THE PLANE

It's one thing to have faith

and another matter entirely

to act on your faith.

Your faith becomes meaningful to you and effective for your salvation only when you have faith in God. But what if you never act on that faith? How meaningful and effective is it then? Look at it this way. Let's say you made a reservation to fly to Hawaii. When the day for your flight arrives, you drive to the airport, check in, and walk to your gate. But rather than taking your seat on the plane, you sit in the airport and watch the plane take off. Then you turn to some guy next to you and say, "Hey, you see that plane? I have a reservation for that flight. My reservation is going to Hawaii."

Your faith in God is like that reservation to Hawaii. Just as you fulfill your reservation to Hawaii by getting on the plane, you fulfill your faith in God by getting with His plan (Ephesians 2:10).

Faith that doesn't show itself by good deeds is no faith at all—it is dead and useless. JAMES 2:17 NLT

DIVINE DESIGN

Don't make plans and then ask for the Lord's

approval. Ask God to direct your planning.

Teenagers quickly learn that it is easier to ask forgiveness than to ask permission. If they ask for permission first, their request may be denied. So they go ahead and do what they want, and they are later prepared to say: "I'm sorry. I didn't know I shouldn't have done that."

If we are honest with ourselves, we often take the same approach with God. We make our plans for what we want, and we leave God totally out of the planning process. After all of the choices have been made, then we involve God by asking Him to "bless" what we have already decided to do.

Don't treat God like a magic wand that you wave over your plans. Involve Him in the decisions of your life at the very beginning. Let Him direct you (instead of the other way around).

START THE IGNITION

The next time you feel weak in the

knees, try using them to pray.

Prayer is a powerful tool because it activates the power of God in your life. God is always with you through the presence of the Holy Spirit, but He won't unleash His power unless you ask Him to, and the way you ask is through prayer (John 16:24). Think of your life as a car (you choose what kind of car you want to be). God is the engine that powers you, and the Holy Spirit is the fuel. But unless you turn on the ignition by praying, you're going to sit there, nice to look at, but going nowhere. Prayer is like the spark that ignites the Holy Spirit to drive God's power.

Oh, and there's one more aspect to our illustration. You'll need a road map to tell you where you need to go. That would be the Bible—God's personal atlas for your life. Don't leave home without it.

Avoiding Temptation

You are less likely to fall into temptation

if you don't walk along the edge.

We all struggle with temptation. When we yield to it, we usually blame it on our weakness. But it's not always a matter of weakness. Sometimes it is just a matter of plain stupidity. We stupidly put ourselves in the path of temptation when we could have avoided it altogether.

Start being smart about resisting temptation. If you know that you are having difficulty with a particular sin, then arrange the circumstances of your life so that you aren't confronted with the temptation as often. Decide ahead of time what you won't do, where you won't go, and what you won't watch. You might even have to disassociate with a few "friends" who are leading you into trouble.

The hardest time to resist temptation is when you're knee-deep in it. It's just a lot easier to stay away from it to begin with.

So humble yourselves before God. Resist the Devil, and he will flee from you. JAMES 4:7 NLT

SETTLE FOR BEST

When you feel like settling

for less than the best,

think about what God wants for you.

There will come a day when you realize that God wants more for you than you could possibly want for yourself. Maybe you've come to that day already, but if not, here's what will happen. As you focus on God daily by reading His Word and talking with Him through prayer, you are going to gain a greater appreciation for who God is and what His will is for you each day. You will recall what God has done in every detail of your life as you eagerly learn how God wants to build your character and use you to impact the lives of others.

At that point you will realize that God doesn't just want you to "get by" each day. He wants you to live your life fully here on earth while you anticipate the amazing life waiting for you in heaven.

"For I know the plans I have for you," says the LORD.

"They are plans for good and not for disaster, to give you

a future and a hope." JEREMIAH 29:11 NLT

APPOINTMENTS TO KEEP

In the morning

you will see the glorious

presence of the LORD.

EXODUS 16:7 NLT

We all carry appointment calendars. Some of us have day planners, and others can't go anywhere without their Palm Pilots. A few even have assistants to help them sort out their appointments and tasks. Why all the fuss? So we can stay on task and keep our appointments. We don't want to miss out on anything or anyone that would help improve our lives. Neither do we want to disappoint anybody who wants to meet with us.

That said, does it seem like a good idea to put God at the top of your appointment list? Of course it does. He's the most important person in the world to you, and His plans for you are the most important tasks. Seek God and what He wants for you every day, and to help you remember, put His name in your appointment book. That's one daily meeting you don't want to miss.

DECLARE YOUR DEPENDENCE

The heavens tell of the glory of God.

The skies display his marvelous craftsmanship.

PSALM 19:1 NLT

The Declaration of Independence happened long before 1776. In fact, humankind declared its independence from God in the Garden of Eden when Adam and Eve believed the lie that they could live independent of God. Since then, we humans have been constantly struggling to do it our way.

God knows that true independence is impossible. There's no way we can function effectively if we are cut off from His help. We are like branches in a vineyard. Once cut off, we die. Jesus is the true vine (John 15:1), and unless we are connected to Him, we will never truly be productive. And our so-called independence won't lead to freedom but to our own destruction.

"Remain in me, and I will remain in you.
For a branch cannot produce fruit if it is severed from
the vine, and you cannot be fruitful apart from me."

JOHN 15:4 NLT

FINISH WHAT YOU START

People will be more impressed

by what you finish than by what you start.

How we love to start stuff! We begin a project with energy as we envision the wonderful result. We enter into a new relationship with enthusiasm as we anticipate the rewarding experience. But sometimes the project bogs down or the relationship sours, and rather than taking things to their proper conclusion, we quit. (Of course, we don't use the word "quit." We prefer to say we "lost interest.")

Jesus once told a parable about what it means to start something. Whatever it is, we need to see it through, or else we shouldn't start in the first place. The principle applies to material things and relationships, especially our relationship with God. Jesus was real blunt about this. God isn't something to sample and then discard when we lose interest. We are to take Him seriously and believe that when we begin our relationship with Him, we need to see it through.

COMPLIMENTS

Thoughtful compliments wear better

than impulsive flattery.

You are wary of insincere friendships, and we don't blame you. So many people bring ulterior motives into a friendship. It is hard to know whether they are really interested in you as a friend, or whether they just want to get something from you or sell something to you. Skepticism is natural if the dinner party turns into a pitch for membership in a Yugoslavian time-share resort.

You can pave the way for meaningful friendships if you dispense with flattery. It is always shallow and usually transparent. It creates an atmosphere of insincerity in the relationship.

Make your conversation count. Learn to give compliments that are meaningful and appropriate. A legitimate, sincere compliment shows that you are aware and appreciative of someone else's effort. That is the stuff on which real friendships are built.

KEEP READING

Leaders are readers.

Everyone wants to follow a leader who is informed and wise, but nobody wants to follow a leader who is a know-it-all. There is a substantial distinction between the two types. Wise leaders know that they can learn from others. The know-it-alls think that there is nothing that others can add to their vast storehouse of knowledge.

Effective leaders are anxious to gain insights from other sources. This usually means reading books and articles on the subjects that are relevant to their responsibilities. The Bible is the best book for this purpose. It deals with the dynamics of personal relationships, and that is what leadership is all about.

If you are in a position of responsibility, make the Bible your leadership manual.

ON INVESTMENTS

Spend more of your time and energy

investing in people

than you do investing in things.

A good investment is determined by the safety of your capital and the rate of return. If you are going to put your money into something, you want to make sure that it won't be lost and that you'll be paid a good dividend.

These same principles apply to the investment of your time and energy. Don't waste your valuable time with frivolous endeavors. Put your effort where it will count and pay off. You may receive the best return on your investment when you put time into other people. You can invest in them through acts of kindness and thoughtfulness. You aren't likely to see monetary returns on your investment, but you are guaranteed spiritual rewards because your good deeds honor God Himself.

Don't just pretend that you love others.

Love each other with genuine affection, and

take delight in honoring each other.

ROMANS 12:10 NLT

IF NOT US, WHO?

Trust God to direct
the circumstances of your
life even if you don't know
what He's doing.

In a time of crisis, an American president gave this charge to the nation: "If not now, when? If not us, who?" It was an inspiring phrase, but not original. The Bible records an event in 479 B.C., when a beautiful Jewish woman named Esther became queen of Persia. It was no accident. God arranged the circumstances of her life in order to elevate her to a high position, and then He used her to save His people.

Whenever you are promoted to a higher position—whether it's in your job, at school, or in the community—you need to recognize that God has put you there for a reason. You may not know right away, but you have to trust God that His timing is perfect, and you need to stay humble with the knowledge that He wants to use you to serve and influence others and glorify Him.

LOYALTY

"The greatest love is shown when people lay down their lives for their friends."

JOHN 15:13 NLT

There is a big difference between acquaintances and friends. Acquaintances are people that you know. They pop into your life (whether you want them to or not) as the result of your circumstances. So, you have acquaintances at work, in your neighborhood, and at church. These are people who may be very nice, but your relationship with them is defined more by contact than by commitment.

One characteristic that distinguishes acquaintances from friendship is loyalty. Friends are committed to each other. They are willing to make personal sacrifices for each other. They don't keep score of who owes a favor to whom. If you have true friends, then thank God for them. They are rare commodities. If you need to increase your friendship network and find a few, then start by being the kind of friend you would want to have.

RIGHTS VS. RESPONSIBILITIES

You are responsible to God

to become what God has made it possible

for you to become.

Political groups and social organizations like to talk about the "rights" of their members. They want the full entitlement to the benefits that are rightfully theirs. Rights are all about "me, me, me."

That is not the attitude God wants you to have. He wants you to forget about your rights and focus on your responsibilities. He wants you fully engaged in helping others. Responsibilities are all about "you, you, you."

God wouldn't be a very popular politician in our society. Most people want to be served and enjoy their privileges. God calls us to be submissive and put the interests of others above our own. It is possible only if God can change your attitude. Are you willing to let Him?

STAY AT IT
EVERY DAY

Discipline begins with small things done daily.

Mark Twain said: "The secret of getting ahead is to get started. The secret of getting started is breaking your complex tasks into small manageable tasks, and then starting on the first one." Good advice, whether you want to finish a short-term project, or you desire to get good at something over a long period of time.

Knowing God doesn't happen over night; it takes a lifetime. And it starts with one small task (such as reading the Bible for say, fifteen minutes each day). Remember: the heart of discipline is repetition, not completion. Don't be discouraged if you don't "get ahead" as soon as you would like. On the other hand, don't just discipline yourself for the sake of discipline. Have a goal in mind—such as knowing God better—so that your daily regiment takes on meaning.

About the Authors

BRUCE BICKEL spent three weeks as an aspiring actor before spending twenty years as a perspiring attorney. His flair for theatrics goes to waste in his law practice (he specializes in estate planning and probate), but Bruce is a gifted communicator. His speeches, seminars, and sermons serve as the outlet for his pent-up comedic and dramatic talents. Bruce resides in Fresno, California, with his wife, Cheryl. When he isn't doing lawyer stuff, Bruce is active at Westmont College, where he has taught and serves on the Board of Trustees.

STAN JANTZ has been involved with Christian retail for more than twenty-five years and currently works in public relations for Berean Christian Stores. Stan and his wife, Karin, live in Fresno, where Stan is active in his church and with Youth for Christ. Stan serves on the Board of Trustees of Biola University.

Bruce & Stan have cowritten twenty-five books, including the international best-seller *God Is in the Small Stuff*. Their passion is to present truth in a clear, concise, and casual manner that encourages people to connect in a meaningful way with the living God.